Make it Happy

CRAFT AND COLOR DESIGNS

by Annie Lang

Ready to use timeless designs and fun for all ages!

You'll find 21 full page vividly colored whimsical designs chosen
from Annie Lang's most popular character images library
to use for your creative DIY projects You'll also find the line art
patterns for each of the designs that you can trace, transfer and
color any way you please. Whether it's a tote bag, wearables,
canvas art or papercrafts, the sky's the limit when you work with
professional designs and patterns. So go ahead and get
your Creative Adventures started and we'll share a few smiles
along the way!

Transferring the linework designs

Trace the design of your choice with pencil and tracing paper. Place transfer paper under the tracing paper and place onto your selected surface. Hold in place with tape if necessary. Retrace over the linework to transfer the design onto the project. For fabrics, trace the design, flip the pattern over and retrace the lines using a fabric transfer pen. Follow manufacturer's direction to iron the design onto your chosen fabric item.

Color or paint these designs with

Craft paints, watercolors, markers, coloring pencils, chalks, inks, fabric pens, paint pens, or crayons

These designs are great for

Home Dec Items like furniture, cabinets, accent items, walls, lamps, glassware, kitchen accessories, office and desk items, bathroom accents, cabinets, patio pots and outdoor items, etc.
Fabric and wearable items like t-shirts, sweatshirts, aprons, canvas shoes, totes, quilting squares, table linens and napkins, window and shower curtains, pillows, etc.
Paper Craft Projects like greeting cards, scrap page elements, tags, labels, stationery items, ornaments, gift bags, etc.

For more ideas and designer tips, please visit my Blog at
http://annielang-anniethingspossible.blogspot.com/
My Pinterest Board at http://www.pinterest.com/anniethings/
or my Facebook Page at
http://www.facebook.com/anniethingspossible

Let's Make Something FUN!

JUST
BEE
HAPPY

JUST
BEE
HAPPY

I AM
AWESOME

I AM
AWESOME

BOOKWORMS

know stuff!

BOOKWORMS
know stuff!

Let's have a
BBQ

Let's have a
BBQ

COOL

COOL

LET'S DANCE!

LET'S DANCE!

FUN IN THE SUN

FUN IN THE SUN

Happy
Little
ME!

Happy
Little
ME!

Happy is as happy does

Happy is as happy does

Honey Bunny

Honey Bunny

Life's a
HOOT

Life's a
HOOT

HUGS

HUGS

hug me!

hug me!

GiMMEE
A
HUG!

GiMMEE
A
HUG!

GIMMEE
A
HUG!

GIMMEE A HUG!

Monkeyshine
time

Monkeyshine
time

SHINE ON!

SHINE ON!

Space
racer

Space
racer

think
Sunny
thoughts

think
Sunny
thoughts

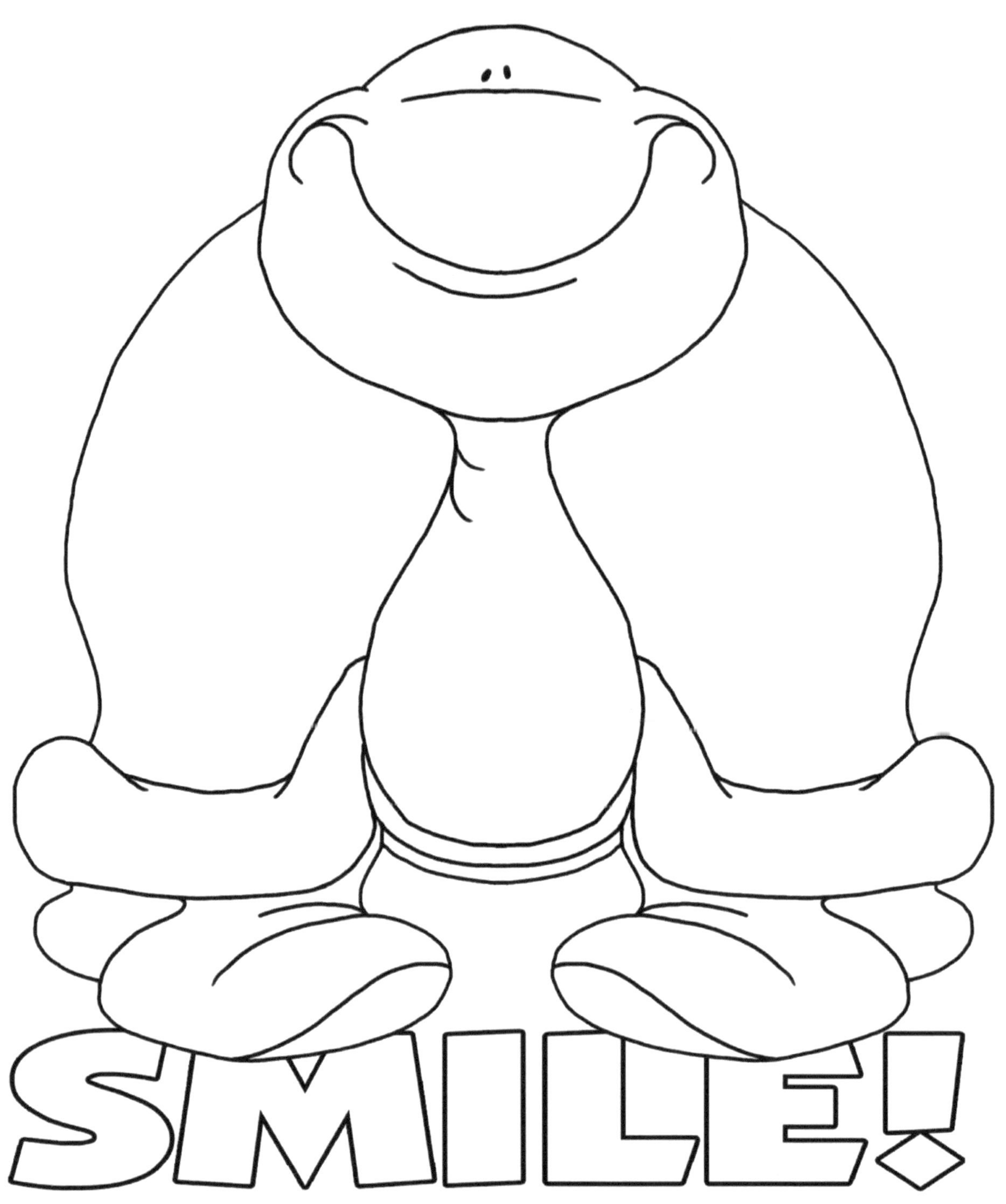

SMILE!

SMILE!